From Content to Book Draft:
Tips On How To Write Your First Book

NONNAC CONTENT & PRESS

For information: AuthorS.W.Cannon@gmail.com

www.AuthorSWCannon.com

ISBN- 978-0-9895183-1-4

1. Non-Fiction 2. Self-Help 3. How-To 4. Guide 5. Motivational

Cover Design by S. W. Cannon with photography by D. Jerome Smedley

Dedication

This book is dedicated to all the writers on their journey to becoming first time authors and the value they will bring to the world with their first book.

I see you. I was you. I'm here to help you.

#HappyWriting

Acknowledgements

I acknowledge my family for making the sacrifice of my time as I worked on my passion of helping authors.

I acknowledge the never-ending support of my book club In The Company Of Twelve (ITC12) in Birmingham, Alabama. Even when I showed up to meetings without having read that month's book, they were understanding and supportive of my big picture.

I acknowledge Tasha "TC" Cooper of Upward Action® (**www.UpwardActionMedia.com**) for creating the opportunity for me to sharpen my author coaching skills with the ACTIONeer book challenge.

I acknowledge the ACTIONeers that took part in the book challenges and affirmed for me that my superpower works. Thank you Dr. Nicola Brown, Allison Cain, Eddie Colson, Felicia Padilla Dowe, Lee Farmer, Susan Fish, Dr. Zoe Fludd, Jamal Hardman, Jason Hodge, L. Denise Jackson, Angelique Y. Johnson, LaMeél Kimsé, Patricia Bias Morrison, Decoda Roberts, Dawn E. Stephens, Patrick Dewayne Stewart, and Gwen Watts.

I acknowledge Dr. Will Moreland (**www.WillMoreland.com**) for polishing my genius with his endless motivation and experience.

Testimonials

AWESOME! It is pretty incredible what SW Cannon can do in less than 30 days! As a result of SW Cannon's knowledge, expertise and exceptional skills I am well on my way to becoming the author I always dreamed I could be. *For all those who may have a desire to become an author and may not be sure how or where to start, SW Cannon should be the first person you contact. Believe me, you will not be disappointed.*
 -Zoe Fludd, Ph.D., M.S.W., GEORGIA

I'm a novice author who has always had plenty of ideas and a love for writing, Luckily, I was introduced to SW Cannon and she held my hand through the steps of actually writing the proper way. *She also helped me overcome writer's block.* The greatest advice she gave me was "write what you know."
– Melvin Stringer, ALABAMA

SW Cannon of Nonnac Content & Press is very personable with her coaching style. I say this because she was consistent in reaching out to me to keep me on track, in a non-overwhelming way when I fell behind due to being under the weather. *She displayed empathy towards my situation but still held me accountable for my deadline to be on the right path in writing my book detailing 7 Ways to Create Happy Customers Who Spend More.* That I believe is going above and beyond. -Decoda (Mee) Roberts, MASSACHUSETTS [LivingNowForLater.com]

I was so lucky to meet Sha' through an online, month-long book-writing challenge. Sha' provided a wonderful level of guidance, inspiration and encouragement to the group and I'm sure her consistent presence was appreciated by all. Most importantly for me, she picked up on a major stumbling block which could have prevented me from reaching my goal. Her gentle, considerate suggestions had me thinking more flexibly and - more importantly - gave me a sense of optimism again. *As a result, that stumbling block dissolved and I reached what had seemed an unattainable goal of writing a book draft within a month.* Thanks so much Sha', your support made a huge difference to me! - Nicola Brown, NEW ZEALAND

Testimonials

I reached out to Ms. Cannon in April 2014, during a time when my ideas for writing had become overwhelming. She coached me over the phone sharing her wealth of knowledge and encouraging me to follow my dream of writing. I will be honest, I didn't think a published author would give me the time of day, but Ms. Cannon did and she also followed up with me via text and Facebook inbox messaging. I am truly thankful for her willingness to guide me toward my ultimate writing goal. *I find myself jotting down notes, recording my thoughts on my voice recorder and making journal entries all thanks to following simple tips from Ms. Cannon.* Thanks again and "Happy Writing." - Bridget Gooden, ALABAMA

I met and had the pleasure of working with SW Cannon as a writing coach for a Facebook writing group. She provided invaluable information from start to finish. *She helped me to narrow down my focus as I was moving through the process. Every day she had tips that helped me better understand and frame what I was doing.* For example she told us to add a bit of ourselves -a more personal touch- to our writing. That tip sent me back to my introduction to share more of my personal experiences and in doing so, gave the introduction and the devotional much more depth. Because of my experience with SW Cannon, I am going to connect with her to help me with the rest of the publishing process. - Patricia Morrison, ARKANSAS

I've been years playing around with the idea of writing a book... It wasn't until being in a broadcast with Sha' "SW" Cannon, Tasha "TC" Cooper, and Dr. Will Moreland, that I was encouraged to pull the trigger! *Sha' gave of her expertise, as a published author, to guide us in the direction to completion, with templates, feedback, and the support first time authors uniquely require.* I'm grateful to say that I am now the author of "Media Planning Your Non Profit Funding Vehicles - Simple Tips To 'Profit' Your Non-Profit Organization" – Jason Hodge, WASHINGTON **http://TheJasonHodge.com/firstbook-shab**

Mind Your Business

"If you believe it will work out, you'll see opportunities. If you believe it won't, you will see obstacles." — Dr. Wayne Dyer

An enormous amount of people say they are going to write a book. The percentage that actually does write a book is very low. Why did some succeed and others not? Is it because their content was better? Is it because *they* were better? No. It is because their mind set was better!

Anytime you decide to do anything, your success will depend on whether YOU think YOU can do it. People that are positive about what they know aren't easily swayed. With that in mind, people that know they will complete what they set out to do will not be stopped by obstacles either large or small.

If you cannot commit to writing and not stopping until it is completed…

If you cannot make writing a priority to the extent that sacrifices are made to create time to routinely write until you have finished…

If you think that you are NOT a worthy messenger for your subject matter and therefore unworthy of being a published author…YOU WILL **<u>NOT</u>** COMPLETE YOUR BOOK! *STOP NOW AND COME BACK WHEN YOUR MIND BELIEVES!*

<u>NOTES</u>

Before You Begin

"What you need to do is the hard work day by day in building a group of people who trust you, and want to support you when it's time." — Seth Godin

People tend to believe becoming an author starts when the pen hits the paper or words are typed on the screen. Truth is, your journey as an author should begin before you start to write. Building an AUTHOR PLATFORM should be your first step. Unless you have a publishing company willing to spend thousands of marketing dollars on your launch once your book is published, you have to begin to create buzz about your book now. What is an author platform? The word *platform* means a raised level surface on which people or things can stand. As an author, you need to be raised where people can see you. Rise by nurturing awareness of your book, while building a relationship with your target readers now.

Social Media is definitely the great equalizer between self-publishers, small publishers, and large, well-known publishing houses. It doesn't take a marketing genius to cultivate social media and create what I call a *Google Footprint*. This footprint is created when your web presence as an author comes up in the Google search listing for your name. The more places your name as an author can be found on the internet, the larger your Google Footprint will become.

Let's grow your footprint:

- create a Facebook account for your author name;
- create a Twitter account for your author name;
- create a LinkedIn account for your author name; and
- create an author website.

If you already have some of the social media

accounts listed, you may change the account names to your author name or simply add the title author in front of your name. BUT, ask yourself if your current followers are your target readers. It's best to start a new account and attract your target readers so that your attempts to connect are not in vain.

This may seem like a lot to maintain, however there is technology that can help you automate content for some of these accounts. Hootsuite and Dynamic Tweets are two such technologies available at the time of publication for this book. A few of these accounts will not require any or little maintenance once fully created. Another way to raise your platform is to register with Good Reads for an author profile. Then go a step further and add a few original quotes to the Good Reads site. If you are not camera shy, consider the following to add to your arsenal: Periscope account, Meerkat account, Blab account, and/or a YouTube Channel.

How are you using all of these outlets? Start talking about your book. Take your followers on the journey with you while you are writing the book. Introduce your followers to your characters, tips or steps. Create a rapport that will lead to a pool of ready-made potential readers for your book upon completion.

The most natural thing you can do to get the word out about your book is to speak up. Whenever the opportunity arises, appropriately share that you are writing a book, what it will be about and how anyone interested can obtain a copy in the format of their choice once you are done.

If you would like more information on building

your author platform, please check out and connect with me at **www.AuthorSWCannon.com/connect** to stay updated on the availability of information products on the subject.

<u>NOTES</u>

Getting Started

"Success doesn't just happen. It's planned for." — Anonymous

Before any big undertaking, a plan should be formulated. A plan saves time and headaches, as well as provides a guide for completion. Unfortunately, there are many people who start out writing a book and never finish. Life will happen, obstacles will present themselves, and any host of things that will make writing difficult will appear. When you have a plan, you have a map to aid in your success. In writing, the first powerful tool for your plan is to have a book outline. If you create the skeleton for your entire book, it will take less time to add the meat. You will never have to waste time wondering what comes next. With your outline, you are less impacted by writers block and other content creation problems because you already know what you will write about at each step. A bare bones chapter outline template has been added at the end of this chapter for your use. Even better would be to add details, ideas, thoughts and reminders related to your content for each chapter.

In addition to an outline, write a book synopsis. In this second step, you will create the pitch or elevator speech for your book. If someone asks you what your book is about, you should have something ready that sums up the value or the plot of your book. Write this summary down. As you are writing the summary along with your outline, will serve to keep you on track. The great thing about this summary is that it can later be used on the back of your book, on marketing materials and on Amazon or anywhere your book will be sold, to let readers know what your book is about.

The third step in your plan for success is to plot out when you will write. Odds are you are not a fulltime writer that makes ends meet with your written works....yet. Some of you are parents, a spouse, a caretaker of family, have a fulltime job, have a fulltime class schedule, etc... It is best to commit yourself to specific times of the day or week to write. We are most likely to make time for what is planned and scheduled.

Come up with the optimum time to write and then come up with a backup time to write. The backup time is the Plan B for when your optimum time to write falls through. For example, my optimum time to write is after dinner, before my bedtime. My house is quiet and I will have fewer interruptions. However, if I had to work late or my son has a sporting event, then I would most likely be behind on my household duties by the time I make it home. My Plan B is to get up early the next day and write to take the place of the time I did not write the night before.

Take advantage of small chunks of time throughout the day to write instead of only waiting on longer periods of time. To create more or longer periods of writing time, consider giving up time wasters like television, social events, personal social media time, etc… to make more time to write.

The fourth and final step in your plan to successfully finish writing your book is to find a place to write. I have an office and when I am in my office; my family knows not to bother me. However, I haven't always had this distraction-free space to get my writing done. It's also not the only place that I write.

Find a primary space within your home to write. This spot should have few distractions and should be unwelcoming to life's interruptions. Utilize an area without a television or without a television that is on in the area. Be sure that is free from busy foot traffic, quiet enough for your thoughts to be loud, and where you will be comfortable. The perfect place to write may be in your house or in your office at work. There have been times where it was quiet at my job and I was able to crank out a chapter or two during my lunch hour. Get creative, you may find the perfect space on the front porch or in the yard. There are other places to write such as the library, a coffee shop, a friend or family member's house, or a quiet spot on a blanket in the park. Find your sweet spot.

Create your book synopsis; the elevator speech for what your book is about. This is what can later be used on the back cover of your book and any platform utilized to sell your book. For now this summary will serve as a "big picture model" to keep your writing focused on what the book is about as a whole. The goal is to stay true to this synopsis while you write.

BOOK SYNOPSIS

_____

_____

_____

_____

_____

Do NOT focus on quantity of pages and instead focus on quality of information. Break down all concepts and give simple explanations to teach what you want your reader to learn. Along the way ask yourself the following questions to stay on track: Is this the simplest explanation? Could this concept be better explained in two chapters rather than one chapter? Would someone who knew nothing about my content be able to understand what I've written? Did I skip any steps? Did I use undefined, industry jargon or speak over the head of someone without knowledge of the subject? Now plot out, chapter-by-chapter the map to understanding your subject matter.

OUTLINE

Chapter Title

_____

Chapter Brain Storm Nuggets

_____

_____

_____

_____

OUTLINE
(Continued)

Chapter Title

_____

Chapter Brain Storm Nuggets

_____
_____
_____
_____

Chapter Title

_____

Chapter Brain Storm Nuggets

_____
_____
_____

Chapter Title

_____

Chapter Brain Storm Nuggets

_____
_____
_____

Page ___

NOTES

OUTLINE
(Continued)

Chapter Title

_____

Chapter Brain Storm Nuggets

_____

_____

_____

Chapter Title

_____

Chapter Brain Storm Nuggets

_____

_____

_____

Chapter Title

_____

Chapter Brain Storm Nuggets

_____

_____

_____

Page ___

Created by Nonnac Content & Press: Providing Tips & Tools To Inspire and Create Better Writers

<u>NOTES</u>

The eBook and self-publishing industries have revolutionized acceptable book length standards. An eBook can be any number of pages, even as few as 10 or 20 pages. With authors now taking back the ownership of their work through self-publishing, they and not the publishers are dictating the lengths of their books in all genres. The new trend is quick reads packed full of good information or a great story.

There are many word processing programs out there for typing your book. I utilize the tried and true Microsoft Word program. The word count is shown at the bottom left corner of the screen in a Word document. The total is the accumulated total thus far, including any miscellaneous pages like the title page, forward, etc... To get the word count of a specific area of words, simply highlight that area and the word count will appear at the bottom left corner of the screen with a smaller number, a forward slash and then a larger number. The smaller number is the word count for the selected area and the larger number is the word count for all words in the document (575/20,783). Or depending on your version of Word, it could display as '575 of 20,783' with the first number being the number of words within the chosen area and the second number being the total number of words for the entire document.

Start writing your book with the end in mind. Format your Word page size to fit that of the size of your desired printed book page and you have a good measure of how many pages your book will be upon its printing. More tips to help you envision the finished, printed version of your work are as follows: the odd page numbers should appear on the right side of a two page view and the even page numbers should appear on the left side of a two page view, therefore your first page of actual content for your printed book should be on the right side of a two page view. This two page view is consistent with your view if you were opening a physical book. Tradition says the first page of each new chapter should start on the right side (even if a blank page is used on the left of the new chapter page to push it to the right side).

A related tip: if your book is too lengthy; consider splitting the book into smaller volumes as not to cut into your profit later in the publication process. The longer your book, the higher the wholesale cost and the smaller the profit margin between the whole cost and retail price.

NOTES

Nugget Collection

"Ideas come from everything" — Alfred Hitchcock

Before you begin writing and all throughout the writing process, content ideas will come. This is your genius at work. It is imperative that you have a system for storing these loose nuggets. The brain is amazing, it will come up with new ideas at any given time and we have to be ready to record them for use at a later date. Especially use nugget collection when you are writing one book and an idea for another book comes to you.

When you aren't able to sit in your sweet spot at your designated time to write, here are a few ways you can collect your valuable nuggets:

1. send a text message to yourself
2. email yourself
3. keep a notepad with you at all times designated only for your writing ideas

Don't have time to write or it's simply too inefficient and inconvenient? Try these tips:

1. leave yourself a voice message
2. use a voice recorder app to dictate messages to yourself
3. dictate directly into a text message, email or word processing document (most efficient of the three)

When dictating or transcribing voice recordings, be sure to use a separate document to store your nuggets rather than use your book draft document. When you are ready to use your nuggets, simply cut them from the nugget storage document, paste them into your book draft document and clean it up as needed.

Whatever it takes, find a way to capture your ideas while you're out and about. To go a step further, I organize my ideas by categorizing them. A few of my categories are: blog ideas, new book ideas, and chapter ideas for a current book.

NOTES

Only You Can Be You

"Today you are you! That is truer than true! There is no one alive who is you-er than you!" - Dr. Seuss

Make sure that you find ways to include your personality in your content. You may not be the first to write about your topic for non-fiction or to use the plot that anchors your fiction, but YOU are what is different from what is already out there.

A great way to infuse yourself into your content is by creating original quotes or buzzwords to sprinkle throughout. Another great way is to tell the reader how to use the tools and tips that you give through sharing your life experience. Yet another way is sharing by way of anecdote. This is a wonderful way to personalize non-fiction content. Personalizing the information can give more substance and understanding to your reader in fiction as well. Use relatable situations that conjure a better mental picture of your content. Inject an emotional response by giving your character's feelings the description of how you would feel if what happened to your character were to happen to you. Include what you were told about the impact of that situation by someone else who went through it. Both descriptions will give your reader a more relatable and memorable experience while reading your book. These are the books that readers enjoy the most and tell their friends about.

NOTES

MUAH K.I.S.S. The Reader

"So the writer who breeds more words than he needs, is making a chore for the reader who reads."

— Dr. Seuss

Whether you are writing fiction or non-fiction, as an author your goal is to have your readers follow and understand your writing. K.I.S.S. is the acronym for the philosophy of simplicity and it stands for 'keep it simple stupid'. Although you aren't stupid, it isn't smart to over complicate your content.

Be clear and concise with your wording. The fewer words used to express a thought, the better. Keep your information in the simplest form. If it can be misinterpreted, it will be. A confused reader is an unhappy reader. In non-fiction you are the teacher and the reader is the student, make sure your information is organized in a way that the reader can learn from it straightforwardly. In fiction, do not ramble along to add pages to your book. As discussed earlier in this book, quantity of pages does NOT hold more value than quality of information for non-fiction or the quality of well-structured entertainment for fiction books.

Another way to simplify content is to include helpful tools within your book. For non-fiction, it really takes your expertise from research (reading the book) to application (performing the directed actions you've taught them). Include an easy formula or calculation. For example, a way to figure out what your retail price should be based on your wholesale price for the best profit margin. Include the best equipment to use. For example, in a cook book add the fact that the $98 KitchenAid blender does all the work of the more expensive blenders for a lower price. <u>Create and include a helpful template</u>. For example, the book outline included in this book. Providing examples, anecdotes and/or analogies drive your more complicated explanations home by creating a better mental picture of your content. These inclusions to your book will simplify complex concepts and applications to add value to your information thus identifying you as an expert.

For fiction, the right word choices can really help the reader play the movie of your story in their head. If you are writing science fiction and your characters live in a wondrously new place, in addition to describing it, add a map to help direct the visualization of the world you have created for your readers as they read. If your main character is using a tool not known to the average person, define it by relating it to a known tool or include a rendering of that tool to help your reader grasp the new information and move past it to the rest of your juicy plot. If in your story, one of the prominent characters had a memorable routine of drinking tea or eating a certain meal or doing yoga or whatever, to add to the experience of the reader include the recipe or a few yoga positions for them to try for themselves. Fiction writing is all about awakening the senses of the reader as they read. Give them more to see, do and experience for a memorable read.

I cannot say it enough, simplicity is the key. If you write over your readers' heads, then you have devalued your content. Your book is only valuable to a reader that can understand it. Show them, don't just tell them.

NOTES

Where Did It Come From?

"What a good thing Adam had. When he said a good thing, he knew nobody had said it before." – Mark Twain

Too many graphics and/or pictures in your book can drive up print costs. Even if you don't mind the increased print costs due to including pictures, there is still more to consider. Do NOT use pictures or illustrations you did not create without purchasing the right to use them or without express written permission to use them. In most cases, you will have to pay for the right to use copyright protected work. When investing in the right to use copyrighted material, make sure the rights of use that you have purchased match your intended use of the image, photo, or illustration. One way to get pictures to use for blogs and books is to Google "royalty free pictures" for a list of websites that contain royalty free images you can publish. Read the terms of use for these websites carefully. Consult with an attorney as needed.

At the time of publication, my favorite site was **www.Pixabay.com** for royalty free pictures. Here are a couple of resource lists for more royalty free pictures:

- **http://blog.kozzi.com/design/25-free-stock-image-sites/**
- **http://www.digitalimagemagazine.com/featured-article/18-more-free-stock-photo-sites/**

Another free and legally worriless way to use pictures in your book is to take them yourself. If you take a picture, you own it and do not need further permissions to use it in print. However, be carefully with what you take pictures of for use in publication. You cannot take a picture of others' art work, faces, original design, logos, and other recognizably unique works belonging to someone else without express permission.

Research, research, and more research. When setting yourself up as an expert on a given topic, it is imperative that your information be correct and up-to-date. In non-fiction, you have to give credit to the originators of the facts that you are using. Making use of statements and facts from another source could easily be plagiarism. *Plagiarism* is defined as committing literary theft by stealing or passing off the ideas or words of another as your own. Do not forget to site your sources; always give credit for someone else's original results, facts, figures, and work. Also be careful when using quotes from books or lyrics, those are also copyright protected.

In fiction you have to be cautious because most fiction is rooted in real life. There are three main areas of concern:

1. *defamation* (spoken injury/slander or written injury/libel to a living person or organization)

2. *right of privacy* (protection of individuals from having private, embarrassing information published about them that is not "newsworthy" or of "public concern")

3. *right of publicity* (the right of living celebrities to protect their name, likeness or persona from being commercially exploited)

There are basically three classes of people that show up in fiction writing: non-celebrities, living celebrities, and dead celebrities. When writing about real people, keep in mind that anyone can take you to court for anything. However, just because someone feels they have been defamed doesn't mean they actually were defamed. It is tough to prove defamation but the annoyance, and cost of going to court to defend yourself, may or may not feel worth a win in the end.

NOTES

Why Be A Loner

"Writing may be a solitary endeavour, but what writer couldn't use a little support, feedback, and camaraderie?" — Judy Reeves

SUPPORT, we can do little in life without the support of others. As a writer, the best place to receive the industry specific support that you need is to be a part of a writing community. There are a number of ways to do this.

Search for local writing groups that share information amongst each other. Google 'writing group' and add your location (i.e. 'writing group Georgia'). Some of these groups even have readings where you can get feedback on your work. A lot of these groups use the local libraries as a meeting place, so check with the libraries in your area also.

There are also national organizations that sponsor conferences, book selling events, book tours, etc... Now Google 'book event,' 'writing conference,' and 'writers' organization.' A wonderful challenge that has become a community of its own is the National Novel Writing Month challenge ("NaNoWrMo") that takes place every November. If you are interested in participating in this challenge or just finding out more about it, go to **www.nanowrimo.org**.

There are even online groups that you can join. I invite you to join my Nonnac Writing Community at http://NonnacWritingCommunity.website/. Just like other membership sites, there are insightful articles, check lists, and guides and other information of help and interest to writers. However there is also a heavy community aspect that lends itself to engagement with like minds, accountability, collaborations, challenges, Q&As, and opportunities for individual problem solving. That is the true value of the membership. But as if that isn't enough, additionally there are guest gurus, events, incentives, and more.

An easy way to compound the community experience is to follow other writers, publishers, editors, book cover artists, and other people with occupations in the writing industry on social media to see what information they are sharing.

NOTES

Wear One Hat At A Time

"When I'm writing, I make words my b*tch. But when I'm editing, the words make me their b*tch. It all equals out in the end." — Richard B. Knight

When you are writing your book, just write. Do not be distracted by other related duties. The goal is to write to completion FIRST, then worry about editing, flow, bios, dedications, etc…

Complete the meat of your book and start the side dishes when you are done. You are a writer until the book is written. Once the book is written, then you can go back and do a once over to clean it up. Both processes are too significant to combine; they each need their own time and focus.

Many writers take up so much time with everything but the writing, that the most important thing, the book, doesn't get done. Think about the sacrifice you made to find time to write. Don't waste that time on something it wasn't earmarked for and something that isn't the first priority.

As you write, let the content and the organization of the content, be your focus. Use your normal spelling, punctuation, and grammar habits to get the information out.

As a writer, it's hard to "kill your darlings" as Steven King says. The book in its entirety is a writer's baby. It's very hard to cut a finger, arm, or leg away from your own baby. I use Beta Readers to identify what in my content should be deleted, revised or expounded upon. If you know avid readers within your genre, then you may not have to pay for Beta Readers. Make sure to use a diverse group, as different views bring different aspects and more value to the review of your content. My Beta Reader group has men and women of varying races and ages. Their only commonality is they read within my genre often.

It is my stern opinion that someone else should do the final edits to your work. I have a tendency to see what is not there when I read my own work. Why? Because I know how it should read. I read with expectations that may not be fulfilled within the reality of my writing. Before giving my work to my editor, I do my own first round of revisions to submit a best draft copy. Before submitting my draft to my editor, I also remind her of my usual faux paus: unmatched word tense, run-on sentences, switching between points of view, etc... With those reminders, I am less likely to have those mistakes overlooked. Editors, like writers, are not perfect; help them, help you have the best copy of your book possible.

NOTES

Unstoppable

"Don't watch the clock; do what it does. Keep going."
— Sam Levenson

It takes a lot of talent, time and energy to write. However, you are not a published author until you have first completed the writing process and secondly the publishing process.

Life will happen. Important interruptions will erupt. Family, friends, work, health issues, etc… will be obstacles to the completion of your book. Some of these problems will be solved by your writing plan of when and where to write. But it is impossible to come up with a plan for EVERY hindrance that can and will occur. The absolute best tool to fight against failure to complete your book for WHATEVER reason is your internal motivation. If it is what you want, you will not allow anything to stop you. Keep in mind the reason you are writing your book. Stay focused on your end game. You will get there, even if it isn't as soon as you thought.

Not done by the time you thought you would be? Move the deadline. Can't come up with the amount of content that you previous expected? Use the content you have and bring it to a close rather than adding information that takes you further from completion. Instead of focusing on adding missing chapters, focus on bringing the story or content to an end starting from where you are now. Adjust how long you initially estimated your book would be in both your mind and your writing. If it is shorter than you thought, consider naming your chapters rather than numbering them.

Sometimes it takes an adjustment in thinking to

get to the end. You are the captain of this ship, you decide where it goes. Point it toward completion for success. Keep your eye on the prize. YOU CAN DO THIS BUT YOU HAVE TO BELIEVE THAT YOU CAN! Even after dedicating the first chapter of this book of the importance of your mindset, let me say that again: **YOU CAN DO THIS BUT YOU ABSOLUTELY HAVE TO BELIEVE THAT YOU CAN!**

NOTES

Don't Do It

"Master your strengths; outsource your weakness."
— Ryan Khan

First and foremost: IF YOU ARE NOT FINISHED WRITING YOUR BOOK, DO NOT STOP WRITING!

You are a writer. Unless you are using a ghost writer, writing is where your talent lies. Writers are not always good at all of the parts to the whole, when it comes to getting a book ready for publication. Know your strengths and weaknesses for the betterment of your work.

I have previously suggested to you that a writer should not edit their own work. If you are not good with punctuation, grammar, and spelling, then it is not just a suggestion. Do NOT edit your book.

It is said that to write, you must read. If you are not an avid reader, do NOT publish your book without having a diverse selection of readers of your genre read over your content (also see exert on Beta Readers in an earlier chapter for more detail).

If you are self-publishing and have never submitted a book to be printed or published digitally before, do NOT format your own book. Ever see an ebook or print book where the spacing, type set, and/or headings were "off"? You do NOT want those types of mistakes to riddle your book like bullet holes. Confused and distracted readers become brutally harsh critics when reviewing your book.

If you are not a graphic designer or extremely creatively infused, do NOT work on your own cover art. A book cover is the first representation of your book. Any graphics on the cover should relate to the plot or the information therein. A huge cover mistake is having a book cover that is not represented well as a small thumbnail picture. All ebook covers should have a legible title and author name that can be easily read when displayed as a small picture. Book covers are often selected for purchase from a gallery of other mini book covers. Some print books are sold on websites and different online distributors in the same manner. Even if your book is being featured and not sold, there is a chance it could be displayed among other book covers as a thumbnail or have a small picture with text about your book beside it.

I read somewhere that the average book by an unknown author sells no more than 250-300 copies, even if published by a well-known publishing house. That estimate can be with the help of a marketing department. If you would like to sell at least the average amount or a number over the average amount of copies, do NOT attempt to be your own marketing department. If your social media efforts have run dry, hire a marketing expert to leverage your reach and increase the possibility of getting your book into more hands within your target audience.

NOTES

To Self-Publish or Not To Self-Publish

"Authors today need a publisher as much as they need a tapeworm in their guts." — Rayne Hall

I won't even beat around the bush on this one. I am a huge proponent of self-publishing. Call me a control freak but I want to have the last word on how my book cover will look, what my content is about, what will get edited out of my content, how my book will be marketed, etc…

I won't lie to you. When I made the decision to self-publish my very first book, I was afraid. I was afraid that my book wasn't as good as I thought and there would be no one to tell me. I was afraid that I couldn't sell as many copies without the help of a well-known publishing house. But even more terrifying to me than those things was handing over control of all that was important to me regarding this baby I'd breathed life into. Like a parent, I wanted to be responsible for raising it the way I saw fit.

Be careful of some of the publishers out there. I've heard horror stories about authors allowing so-called publishers to publish their books. A fellow author and friend of mine allowed one of these 'publishers' to distribute his book on Amazon as a print book and a Kindle ebook. He gave them his final draft and they "published" it on Amazon. He was happy with the result. Then he started realizing he wasn't getting paid from confirmed sales. When the 'publishing company' stopped being responsive, he also realized there was no way to gain control over the money that came in from Amazon. To add insult to injury, he did not have control over the price set for the book nor the ability to change the price or add a new edition to the book.

THE SOLUTION: Pay to have your book formatted for Amazon print and ebook, then submit it for distribution under an Amazon account that you retain control over. There are no upfront costs to uploading your formatted book and cover art to Amazon for distribution. Much like PayPal, they take a certain amount per book transaction and send you the remaining balance. You can even purchase printed copies of your book at a wholesale price (the cost of printing only, instead of the retail price of your book). The more books you purchase, the less your total wholesale cost for the books.

Horror story number two came from a fellow author I met at a book fair. He displayed and sold his books right next to my booth. Being so close in proximity, we began a conversation. He revealed he paid $3800 for a 'publishing company' to 'publish' his book for distribution on Amazon as a print book only. Within his $3800 package, he was to receive Amazon distribution, 200 printed copies of his book, and a website to promote his book. On the day we attended the book fair, it had been a year since he paid for his package and he still didn't have a website. He also didn't have direct control over his Amazon account to track sales, monitor analytics, and make changes to the book or the price.

THE SOLUTION: Once again, pay to have your book formatted for Amazon print and submitted for distribution under an Amazon account that you control. Pay to receive printed copies of your book in quantities according to your budget or pending opportunities to sell your book inventory. Pay for a simple website. Had he done these things using a la carte services, for the size and format of his book, his out of pocket expense would have been well under half of what he paid in total.

I believe an author should be able to control the destiny of their talent. I believe in self-publishing. The hardest part of the publishing process for a self-publisher is marketing the book to unconnected readers and attaining legal advice for personalized protection. Although these services can be invested in a la cart, it is usually what the so-called 'publishing companies' lack in offering also. This is a huge indicator that you are not dealing with a 'real' publishing company. Instead, they are the middle man increasing the price of the same a la cart services you easily have access to while they keep control of your hard work.

NOTES

Which Way?

"Who exactly seeks out a coach? Winners who want more out of life." — Chicago Tribune

New endeavours are always frightening. The unknown can be easily overcome with a map directing you to a successful route. This is what an author coach can do for you, the first time author; provide a customized map to get you from where you are, to where you want to be.

Do you wish to save time and money on your writing and publishing process through first-hand knowledge gained from personalized guidance on your particular blind spots?

Do you have ideas and content that you need help getting organized for book form?

Is your content missing that UMPH to take it to

the next level?

Prevent the cost and energy of trial and error. Get a coach.

www.AuthorSWCannon.com/Author-Coaching

NOTES

Author *and* Author Coach S. W. Cannon

S.W. Cannon was raised in Alabama but now lives in Georgia. Sha' (pronounced 'shaye') is a published author of both fiction and non-fiction.

She also has freelance experience in copy writing (fashion/style) and content writing (legal field) but her favorite work is within the lifestyle/relationship genre for both the male and female demographics. Add blogger to her credits, as she has a blog on relationships spanning topics for romantic and interpersonal relationships.

S.W. Cannon started helping other indie authors with writing and self-publishing. Her new found passion led her to lend her expertise to more authors with the writing and self-publishing process, so she became a coach.

Are you a first time author? You can do it. She can help: **www.AuthorSWCannon.com/Author-Coaching**